THE
GOD
WHO IS
THERE

LEADER'S GUIDE

THE
GOD
WHO IS
THERE

LEADER'S GUIDE

Finding Your Place in God's Story

D. A. CARSON

BakerBooks
a division of Baker Publishing Group
Grand Rapids, Michigan

© 2010 by D. A. Carson

Published by Baker Books
a division of Baker Publishing Group
P.O. Box 6287, Grand Rapids, MI 49516-6287
www.bakerbooks.com

Printed in the United States of America

Library of Congress Cataloging-in-Publication Data
Carson, D. A.
    The God who is there : finding your place in God's story. Leaders's guide / D. A. Carson.
        p. cm.
    Includes bibliographical references.
    ISBN 978-0-8010-1373-7 (pbk.)
    1. Bible—Study and teaching. 2. Bible—Hermeneutics. 3. God (Christianity)—Study and teaching. I. Title.
BS600.3.C37 2010
220.6′1—dc22   2010021091

In keeping with biblical principles of creation stewardship, Baker Publishing Group advocates the responsible use of our natural resources. As a member of the Green Press Initiative, our company uses recycled paper when possible. The text paper of this book is comprised of 30% post-consumer waste.

Contents

Preface

This brief leader's guide is designed to be used along with *The God Who Is There: Finding Your Place in God's Story* (also published by Baker) and the corresponding video series (available on DVD or, as individual talks, as free downloads at www.thegospelcoalition.org).

What I have tried to do in the main book and the video series is to run through the Bible in fourteen chapters to help those with no knowledge of the Bible, or relatively little knowledge, learn how the Bible "works," how it hangs together—whether the readers of the book or the viewers of the video series are believers or not. Each chapter focuses on one or more passages from the Bible, unpacks it a little, and tries to make connections with the context, drawing the lines together to show how they converge in Jesus. By and large I have presupposed very little prior acquaintance with the Bible.

I should reiterate here what I said in the preface to the larger volume: I do not pretend to be a neutral bystander, coolly weighing what some will think of as the pros and cons of Christian faith. I am a Christian, and what I have found of God in Jesus Christ is so wonderful that I am eager for others to know it too—and to know him.

This leader's guide mirrors the same fourteen chapters that are found in the main book. This guide, however, asks discussion questions, suggests further reading, indicates how the material might tie into broader questions of Christian thought and life, and makes some practical suggestions about how to lead group discussion and answer questions that may arise. An introduction prepares the way for these fourteen chapters with some ideas about how leaders might use this guide to help people profit as much as possible from the series. From time to time I hope to bring out new editions of this guide that benefit from suggestions sent in by those who use it, so please do not hesitate to send such suggestions to me at the Gospel Coalition.

D. A. Carson
Soli Deo gloria

Introduction

I would like to begin by making some suggestions about how to use this leader's guide.

Each of the following fourteen short chapters corresponds to the fourteen chapters in *The God Who Is There: Finding Your Place in God's Story*. The chapters in this leader's guide are divided into several sections:

Discussion Questions

Suggestions for Further Reading

Broader Theological and Pastoral Reflections

Practical Suggestions

How much space will be devoted to each section will vary considerably from chapter to chapter.

I cannot too strongly emphasize that leading Bible studies, not least Bible studies that take participants through the entire Bible, is a skill that can be honed and matured with time and experience. If this is your first time leading such a study, do not be intimidated by the suggestions for further reading or by the additional theological reflections that this leader's guide includes. The section "Discussion Questions" may be all you need or want as you help participants work their way through the material. On the other hand, if you are leading people through this material for the second or third time, you may find it useful to engage in some of the extra reading suggested in this guide. Even then, it will be important not to be intimidated, because most likely you will not have time to read everything that is suggested. That is likely to be undertaken by only the most experienced leaders of Bible studies.

The discussion questions are of several kinds. The first ones in any list solicit answers that show readers have understood the material in the chapter. Some questions drive participants to read certain biblical passages and find answers from the Bible itself. If a question asks for specific biblical content, then the leader should gently encourage participants to be satisfied with answers only if the biblical content is found. "Where did you find that in the text?" or "Does verse such-and-such have a bearing on this question?" are gentle ways of keeping in touch with what the Bible actually says. Later questions in each list require a little more synthesis or reflection on how the biblical passages and themes relate to contemporary culture and even to the individual participants themselves.

Thoughtful, prayerful preparation by the leader is hugely important. Such preparation may well encourage you to substitute some of your own questions for those provided in this leader's guide. No matter how well you have prepared your questions, however, once the dynamic in the group has reached the point where participants trust one another and feel free to bring their own questions, discussion can—and often does!—run in interesting and unpredictable directions. Some suggestions on how to handle such developments:

1. Never let them fluster you. Enjoy the discussion, and love the participants.
2. Prepare far enough ahead in the series that if you can see that a good question really belongs in a later session, you can suggest that the question be brought up there.

3. Where questions are veering off into little set speeches on what the participant thinks about life, God, truth, and the universe, with very little connection to the topic and texts at hand, thank the participant for sharing his or her perspective, but keep quietly reminding folk that this is a series that tries to understand what the Bible says, whether or not anyone believes it.

4. When someone fixates on a relatively minor point that no one else in the group seems to be interested in, suggest that after the public session is over there might be time to talk about this minor point in private, perhaps over a cup of coffee.

5. Never bluff. If you plainly do not know how to answer, admit it frankly and cheerfully, and promise to try to do some homework and find good answers by the next meeting.

The material in this study could be used in half a dozen different ways. Some might prefer to watch the video and then engage in discussion. Others might find it helpful to read the corresponding book chapter, either before or after the video (or, for that matter, without using the video). The series could be used in a small group—in a college dorm Bible study, for example, or in a Bible study group in a local church. In some contexts it might be useful to begin with a meal and general conversation, mingling believers and unbelievers, before embarking on each study.

The German pastor and theologian Helmut Thielicke used to say that there are two kinds of evangelism: Cartesian and kerygmatic. By "Cartesian" he was thinking of approaches to evangelism that begin with "I" and "me"—my needs, hopes, aspirations, guilt, fears—followed by a presentation of how God meets me in my needs. By "kerygmatic" he was thinking of approaches to evangelism that begin by announcing what God has done, often called the *kerygma*. Insofar as *The God Who Is There* is evangelistic, it largely belongs to the latter camp. By unpacking what the Bible actually says about who God is and what he has done, in some ways its chapters are announcing God; they constitute a quiet introduction to God. Nevertheless, the Bible's storyline builds a sense of drama and plot precisely by showing how desperate human needs are and how only God can meet them. In other words, unpacking the Bible is bound to be both Cartesian and kerygmatic (if we stick with Thielicke's categories). However, we must keep in mind an important distinction. Very often when we humans define our needs, challenges, and problems, they are not set out in categories that line up very well with what the Bible says. To put it differently, when the Bible sets out human needs, its analysis, however complex, is finally tied to the way we ought to be relating to our Creator God and then to one another—but frequently that is not how *we* see our needs. So part of a faithful and useful unpacking of the Bible's storyline is to try to show how the Bible's analysis makes sense.

The rest of this introduction is given over to a series of questions and answers. The questions cover a number of preliminary topics; the answers provide some preliminary bibliography. The books and essays suggested in the following paragraphs may help you negotiate early conversations with nonbelievers and untrained believers alike. Some of the books will be volumes you could usefully give to those who ask the questions; others are more advanced treatments that may benefit leaders but are too much to expect of those just starting out. Once again: you do not have to read *any* of the following material to profit from the material in *The God Who Is There* and from this leader's guide, but obviously exposure to some of it may enrich your discussions.

I should add that I have usually not listed commentaries on the biblical texts that are treated in each chapter. Many commentaries are available in English, written at every conceivable level. A standard one-volume Bible commentary is *New Bible Commentary*, edited by D. A. Carson, R. T. France, and J. W. Motyer. For brief notes on available Old Testament commentaries, see Tremper Longman III, *Old Testament Commentary Survey*; the corresponding volume on New Testament commentaries is by D. A. Carson, *New Testament Commentary Survey*. Useful for understanding something about the different literary genres of the Bible and how to understand them is the book by Gordon D. Fee and Douglas Stuart, *How to Read the Bible for All Its Worth*. Of the many specialist volumes, I cannot restrain myself from mentioning Anthony Esolen, *Ironies of Faith*.

(1) What general introductions to Christ and to biblical Christianity do you recommend?

One of the best is still John Stott's *Basic Christianity*. It first appeared in print in 1958. In 2008, InterVarsity Press brought out the fiftieth anniversary edition. Its strength is its simple clarity; its weakness is that it was written when far more people knew something about the Bible and Christianity, so the author could presume on quite a lot of knowledge. Moreover, fewer people were intrinsically suspicious about Christian claims. Today many more people are, frankly, biblically illiterate, so it is important to start farther back and provide more explanations; equally, it is important to dismantle some of the strongest objections many people have to Jesus so that they can better hear what he actually says.

A book written at about the same level, but which takes into account some of these changes, is Peter Jensen's *The Future of Jesus*. Perhaps the best "all-arounder" is Timothy Keller's *The Reason for God: Belief in an Age of Skepticism*. Its strength is that it simultaneously attempts to dismantle what Keller calls "defeater beliefs" while explaining what Christ and the gospel are all about. "Defeater beliefs" are beliefs that defeat other beliefs. For example, if someone holds that there cannot be only one way to God, then if a Christian comes along and insists that Jesus is the only way to God, the Christian's belief is easily dismissed; it has been "defeated" by the prior belief that there cannot be only one way. Keller skillfully unpacks and respectfully dismantles common defeater beliefs while unpacking the gospel.

(2) Are there books that can help me better understand the culture we live in and enable me to be a better discussion leader of the material in The God Who Is There?

Yes, there are many. Part of the challenge, of course, is that in most countries there are many subcultures. One can make some large-scale distinctions—urban, suburban, rural, for example—yet frankly these are not all that helpful. "Urban" includes city-dwellers who are blue-collar workers, others who are yuppies, cities with ethnic neighborhoods (think Chicago), cities where there is more of a melting pot, and so forth. Some residents are very secular, some have Buddhist parents, others are lapsed Catholics, some are observant or non-observant Jews—and on the list goes. The options are so many and so diverse that background reading cannot usefully be prescribed for each of them in a short chapter like this one. With the exception of those relatively rare churches that enjoy teaching ministry so attractive that it draws people in from long distances and several subcultures, the best and most sensitive urban church planting, evangelism, and outreach is neighborhood outreach. Those who lead Bible studies like this one will do best if they know well the people who live in the neighborhoods they serve—or, if these studies are being used on a college campus, they will do best if they know well what makes the students around them tick.

Nevertheless, it is worth noting several studies that chart the beliefs and values of large numbers of young people, not least students, for these are the folk who will grow up to form the dominant opinions of the future. Very useful is the book by Christian Smith and Melinda Lundquist Denton, *Soul Searching: The Religious and Spiritual Lives of American Teenagers*. They coin the acronym MTD: moralistic therapeutic deism. The dominant religion of the teenagers they study is moralistic (lots of rights and wrongs, and you get what you deserve), therapeutic (its purpose is to make you whole and happy), and grounded in a deist's view of God (doubtless he made everything, but he cannot be bothered with the details of our lives). To be aware of how strongly these beliefs are assumed is to be warned about how much will have to be modified by what the Bible actually says. Equally useful are two other books: Jean M. Twenge, *Generation Me: Why Today's Young Americans Are More Confident, Assertive, Entitled—and More Miserable Than Ever Before*; and Richard Kadison and Theresa Foy DiGeronimo, *College of the Overwhelmed: The Campus Mental Health Crisis and What to Do About It*. One need not agree with every argument these authors advance to benefit enormously from their work.

A good popular level analysis of various elements of cultural drift (though the title is a bit apocalyptic) is the book by Marcus Honeysett, *Meltdown: Making Sense of a Culture in Crisis*. On the broader questions raised by the debate on the role of religion and faith in the public square, probably the book to read at the moment is Hunter Baker, *The End of Secularism*, which some are touting as the successor to the older volume by Richard John Neuhaus, *The Naked Public Square: Religion and Democracy in America*. For those wrestling with the different kinds of pluralism that dominate not only Western countries but many others as well, and who find many people to be anti-authoritarian, de-centered, committed to the kind of "democracy" represented by the freedom of the Internet, and suspicious of moral absolutes and of any claim to exclusivism, my book *The Gagging of God: Christianity Confronts Pluralism* has helped some. At a semi-popular level, see Paul Copan, *"True for You but Not for Me": Overcoming Objections to Christian Faith*.

The jury is still out on the long-term effects of the Internet on a whole host of public perceptions. While we have quicker access to a vast array of information, the Internet provides no framework or grid for filtering information, ranking its importance or trustworthiness, or evaluating the credibility of the sources it enables us to find. It builds networks of data-sharers and generates some virtual relationships, but the kinds of relationships developed with time across age groups and ethnicities within the context of a thriving and well-ordered local church are simply out of reach. Perhaps Nicholas Carr is a tad too skeptical when he asks, "Is Google Making Us Stupid?" but it is easy to understand his concerns.[1] While the digital world loves images, the Bible's message is heavily word-centered; while many people hide behind computer screens, the gospel emphasizes relationships between God and people and among people; while many are certain that it is wrong to be certain about very much, Jesus promises certain salvation and pledges a certain hope; while leaders resort to endless self-promotion and marketing strategies, Christians follow a condemned criminal whose most significant hours were spent in agony on a Roman cross.

Learning how Christian doctrines, even difficult doctrines, rightly intersect with the lostness of our generation is part of how we more winsomely articulate the gospel. For example, in predestination God initiates reconciliation and relationships in a generation that does not know how—yet he does so in a fashion that does not feed our wretched narcissism. Quite a few of the theological reflections in the pages that follow attempt to explain in a few sentences how an array of Christian truths rightly impinge on our needy world.

(3) How do I respond to the rising chorus of atheist writings that seem to be garnering a good deal of media attention?

Doubtless the most influential books by the so-called New Atheists are the volumes by Daniel Dennett, *Darwin's Dangerous Idea: Evolution and the Meanings of Life*; Richard Dawkins, especially his *The God Delusion*; Christopher Hitchens, *God Is Not Great: How Religion Poisons Everything*; and Sam Harris, especially his *Letter to a Christian Nation*. M. Z. Hemingway's article "Skepticism, Agnosticism, and Atheism: A Brief History of Unbelief"[2] reminds us that this New Atheism feels contemporary and enjoys a certain popularity but is scarcely all that new: atheism and unbelief have a long history. Moreover, as some historians read the evidence, historians like Alister McGrath argue that we should be commenting on *The Twilight of Atheism: The Rise and Fall of Disbelief in the Modern World*.

Brief but useful responses are found in Ravi Zacharias, *The End of Reason: A Response to the New Atheists* and in R. Albert Mohler Jr., *Atheism Remix: A Christian Confronts the New Atheists*. Gary Habermas has written a good essay reviewing some of the issues, "The Plight of the New Atheism: A Critique,"[3] and William Lane Craig's "Five Arguments for God" refutes Richard Dawkins's *The God Delusion*.[4] Many volumes tackle the New Atheism head on, each from a slightly different perspective. To mention several: David Berlinski, *The Devil's Delusion: Atheism and Its Scientific Pretensions*, devastatingly and sometimes uproariously demolishes claims by scientists that clearly go way beyond the scientific evidence. David Bentley Hart, *Atheist Delusions: The Christian Revolution and Its Fashionable Enemies*, exposes the philosophical and especially the historical errors and misrepresentations of the New Atheists. A courteous, understated, and largely compelling response to some of the philosophical questions is offered by Gregory E. Ganssle in *A Reasonable God: Engaging the Face of the New Atheism*. A fine collection of essays on the subject has been edited by Paul Copan and William Lane Craig, *Contending with Christianity's Critics: Answering New Atheists and Other Objectors*. Bound in one volume are the arguments of both sides, represented respectively by William Lane Craig and Walter Sinnott-Armstrong, *God? A Debate between a Christian and an Atheist*. See also the fast-paced ninety-minute film *Collision: Christopher Hitchens vs. Douglas Wilson*,[5] based on their book *Is Christianity Good for the World? A Debate*. A well-known scientist who writes in a witty, attractive way, Edgar Andrews, has provided us with *Who Made God? Searching for a Theory of Everything*—a book that goes beyond many volumes in this genre in that it goes way beyond arguing for a personal but largely generic "God" but contends explicitly for the God of the Bible, the God who is there.

It is perhaps worth reminding ourselves of some individuals who have abandoned atheism. One remembers the famous remark of Boris Pasternak, the author of *Doctor Zhivago*: "I am an atheist who has lost his faith."[6] More recently, A. N. Wilson, long committed to atheism, wrote a rather moving essay in *New Statesman*, "Why I Believe Again."[7] Similarly, one could point to Antony G. N. Flew, *There Is a God: How the World's Most Notorious Atheist Changed His Mind*.[8] The reason I mention such sources is not that they "prove" anything but that they constitute useful bits of evidence against the claims of the New Atheists that the tide of history is in their favor. As usual, history is a lot messier than many people think.

The reason I have provided this representative bibliography is *not* to turn this series of studies into a debate about atheism and theism, but precisely the opposite: so as to be able to set aside such discussion as much as possible. If participants raise these questions or happily quote one of the New Atheists, it is useful to have in mind several treatments of the subject—something at an easy level, perhaps, as well as something for inquirers, something for those who have been steeped in science or philosophy, and something for troubled Christians. The fourteen chapters of this book do not address such matters directly, only tangentially, for the focus here is to understand what the Bible says about God. Christians hold that the God of the Bible is the God who is there, and in this book we invite both Christians and nonbelievers to see what the Bible says about this God.

(4) Are there other studies that cover ground similar to this book— studies that attempt to survey the whole Bible—that might be useful adjuncts to this one?

There are quite a few of them. At the upmarket end is a book by Craig G. Bartholomew and Michael W. Goheen, *The Drama of Scripture: Finding Our Place in the Biblical Story*. It is organized around the theme of God as king, of the promise and coming of the kingdom. At a more popular level is John R. Cross, *The Stranger on the Road to Emmaus: A Clear and Simple Explanation of the World's Best Seller*. It tends to focus in some detail on several large turning points: creation, fall, exodus, then immediately to Jesus's birth and related narratives, and so forth. Its charts and drawings might make it suitable for use in some Sunday school classes. Its strong commitment to young-earth creationism, and especially its lack of engagement with the assumptions of the postmodern world, will limit its usefulness in some quarters. *From Eden to the New Jerusalem: Exploring God's Plan for Life on Earth* by T. Desmond Alexander is well written and theologically helpful. It starts with Eden and picks up several themes in Genesis 1–3 and in successive chapters runs them forward to the New Testament. Very accessible surveys include Tim Chester, *From Creation to New Creation: Understanding the Bible Story*; Vaughan Roberts, *Turning Points*; and Mark Dever, *What Does God Want of Us Anyway? A Quick Overview of the Whole Bible*. A longer treatment is Colin S. Smith, *Unlocking the Bible Story*, published in four volumes.

If you are working with little children, the best children's Bible storybook now is that of Sally Lloyd-Jones, *The Jesus Storybook Bible*. Do not let the title deceive you: it is not a book of stories drawn exclusively from the Gospels, but the author tries to weave the narrative parts of the Bible together under the rubric "Every story whispers his name."

The God
Who Made Everything

Discussion Questions

1. Summarize what the Bible is, i.e., what kinds of documents make it up.
2. What does Francis Schaeffer contribute to our understanding of the opening chapters of Genesis?
3. What flows from the Bible's emphasis on the fact that God is a talking God?
4. What is the fundamental distinction between Creator and creature—between God as Creator and everything else that exists?
5. What significance is there that the Bible insists that human beings, and human beings alone, are made in the image of God?
6. How does monotheism (belief that there is only one God) shape our outlook and our practice of worship in ways that

are fundamentally different from polytheism (belief that
there are many gods)?

7. How does what the Bible says about creation establish human
responsibility and accountability?

Suggestions for Further Reading

The temptation to write a fifty-page annotated bibliography at
this juncture must be stubbornly resisted. Even cataloguing the
different views that various Christians hold regarding how God
created everything would take many pages. Thus the little coun-
terpoint book edited by J. P. Moreland and John Mark Reynolds,
Three Views on Creation and Evolution, helpful in its own way,
introduces readers to only three important views: young-earth
creationism, old-earth creationism, and theistic evolution. For
people beginning to read in the field, that is a good place to begin,
but the options are considerably more complicated.[1]

In some ways the debates over the age of the earth and of the
universe, though they continue, have been eclipsed by complex and
heated debates over intelligent design. Have traces been left in the
created order of the cosmos that suggest the only adequate explanation for what we see is the hand of an intelligent Designer? Among
the more important of the seminal books that hold this view are
two by Michael J. Behe, *Darwin's Black Box: The Biochemical
Challenge to Evolution* and *The Edge of Evolution: Searching for
the Limits of Darwinism*. One must also read Michael J. Denton,
*Nature's Destiny: How the Laws of Biology Reveal Purpose in the
Universe*. A probing volume that works through the mathemati-
cal probabilities is William A. Dembski, *The Design Inference:
Eliminating Chance through Small Probabilities*. An important
contribution to the literature, written not from the perspective
of biochemistry but from the perspectives of particle physics and
cosmology, is Stephen Barr, *Modern Physics and Ancient Faith*.
A useful history of the movement is Thomas Woodward, *Doubts*

about Darwin: A History of Intelligent Design. For a theological perspective, one might read Christoph Cardinal Schönborn, *Chance or Purpose? Creation, Evolution, and a Rational Faith.*

The debate has become complicated. Perhaps the most important book to allow proponents of both sides to be heard within the covers of one fat volume (805 pages!) is the one edited by Robert T. Pennock, *Intelligent Design Creationism and Its Critics: Philosophical, Theological, and Scientific Perspectives.* Behind many of these debates lurks a knottier one: *What is science?* I shall pick up on this question in the next section. It is enough for the moment to mention four more books. A slightly confrontational but certainly useful book to give to someone who is convinced that science has somehow disproved or buried God is the short book by John Lennox, *God's Undertaker: Has Science Buried God?* Something longer but of the same popular variety is Lee Strobel, *The Case for a Creator.* An excellent short volume for fairly understanding Darwin in his own time and place in history, as well as developments in Darwinism in the ensuing century and a half, is Kirsten Birkett, *The Essence of Darwinism.*[2]

To stand one step removed from these endless controversies and to appreciate positively how creation testifies, as far as the believer is concerned, to some of the attributes of God, one might read the book by Mark D. Futato, *Creation: A Witness to the Wonder of God.* This book picks up on some of the well-known technical data regarding the intricacy of the created order, the astonishingly narrow limits of various ranges of data for the world to be what it is (some of the relevant books were mentioned in the introduction to this leader's guide), and reflects on these data with a helpful *theological* perspective.

Broader Theological and Pastoral Reflections

Here I shall mention four:

First, in the previous section I raised the question, *What is science?* At least three definitions (with many more refinements) currently compete.

(a) Until the nineteenth century, science was simply the state or fact of knowing. What we customarily call science today was then called natural philosophy.

(b) From the nineteenth century on, however, "science" came increasingly to be restricted to knowledge of the natural/material realms and was associated with an array of procedures that included measurement, creation of hypotheses and theories and ways of testing and falsifying them, and so forth. This view of science specified the domain to be studied and known, and, increasingly, the procedures by which such knowledge could be gained—without offering any comment about whether there might be other ways of knowing (for example, from revelation) and even other non-natural/nonmaterial realms that science, so defined, could not properly investigate.

(c) Increasingly, however, "science" is associated with the natural order in the way just described in the point above, but also with exclusive claims about how only science can produce *genuine* knowledge. In other words, science not only becomes associated with philosophical materialism, but it is assumed that science deals with the "real" (material) world of fact and truth while other domains are associated with personal preference, perhaps with "faith" (although, as we shall see later in the main book, faith is never so understood in the Bible).

So where does intelligent design (ID) fit into these diverse definitions? ID claims that the irreducible complexity of biological matter, especially cell life, makes evolutionary development *without* intelligent design a statistical improbability bordering on impossibility; thus intelligent design, and hence an intelligent Designer, seems like the best inference to draw. That inference does not threaten the first of the three definitions of science; it is absolutely anathema to the third, especially if one supposes that the intelligent Designer is a God who by definition stands outside the system of the "natural" order if he is able to design it.

The tricky one is the second definition. ID claims, in effect, that evidence *within* the domain that science (in this second sense) treats, the natural/material world, believably points to the existence of something/someone *beyond* the domain that science (in this second sense) treats. For that reason many scientists are suspicious of the ID movement, claiming it is "not science." Yet ID *is* science in the way that it begins with the natural/material world, collects and sifts evidence, works at the mathematics, and develops a hypothesis; it is *not* science in that its conclusion enters a realm beyond what can be treated by science (in this second sense) alone. Simply to say that ID is "not science," however, seems to concede too much, because the influence of the *third* definition of science invites the conclusion that ID is not about truth or fact but about religious opinions which are tied to mere "faith."

This is not the place to resolve the complicated disputes over the credibility of ID. The only reason I have brought it up is that in my experience it keeps surfacing when you talk with some people about what the Bible says of creation, so it is helpful to know something about it. My own view is that endless discussion about whether ID is "scientific" is fraught with so many semantic difficulties that it is not worth spending a lot of time on the debate unless one is extraordinarily careful to define exactly what one means by "science" and "scientific." At the same time, the accumulating evidence from the physical world that testifies to the wisdom of God and the power of God should not be skirted. It does not constitute "proof" (such that the existence of God is mere inference), but it does constitute powerful witness that must not be ignored.

Second, more important is the observation that all Christians believe the doctrine of creation. In that sense, they are all "creationists." The Bible freed the Roman world from the belief (nicely articulated by Plato in his *Timaeus*) that matter (some sort of primordial clay) is eternal and that a lesser god, the "Demiurge," fashioned that clay much as a potter does to make the world we know. Christians hold that God alone stretches back into eternity past. He made everything else. That truth is foundational; it grounds (as *The God Who Is There* explains) our understanding of the creation's *dependence* on God, including human dependence on God, but it also establishes human significance. We are more than the product of molecules conveniently bouncing around in the primordial ooze. We are creatures made in the image of God, abounding in privilege, with an eternal destiny, accountable to the wise and good Creator who made us. Genesis 1 proclaims a God of power and goodness who so undergirds and upholds the created order that he gives it purpose and meaning.

Third, the better commentaries carefully disclose how interwoven the creation account is. If your Bible study or discussion group has enough time for further exploration, it might not hurt to develop a chart like the following:

Creation Week *(numbers represent the day of the week)*

Problem	Preparation	Population
darkness	1. creation of light	4. creation of sky lights (sun, moon, stars)
abyss of water	2. sky vault, separation of waters	5. sea and sky creatures
initial world is formless and empty	3. dry land and plants: world takes form	6. animals and human beings: world is filled

Careful study of the text makes it possible to unpack how the chapter is put together.

Fourth, to help people understand how a right view of God actually authorizes science, I have sometimes sketched three simple options.

(a) In an "open" universe, commonly adopted in animistic cultures, the relationships between the world and assorted deities are often whimsical. What happens depends on the will and whim of the gods; the business of religion is to find out what placates these gods to make them favorable to you. No science in any modern sense is possible, for the natural world is not sufficiently ordered to discover regular patterns of cause and effect that are tied to the material world itself.

(b) Conversely, in a purely materialist world, all explanations must appeal exclusively to matter, energy, space, and time. Science is possible, of course, but any appeal to God is not. Questions about ultimate origins remain opaque (assuming that speculation about the original mass of the big bang springing forth from nothing is pretty unsatisfactory), and questions of meaning, purpose, beauty, morality, and the like are largely futile and frustrating, despite the best efforts to ground such values in exclusively evolutionary arguments.

(c) In the controlled universe of Christian theism, God remains sovereignly in control of everything, but he operates in an ordered way and often through many secondary causes. Biblical writers know of the water cycle, but they are happy to say that God sends the rain; Jesus knows birds can fall dead from old age, starvation, and disease, but he insists that not a sparrow falls from the heavens apart from his heavenly Father's sanction. The orderliness of God's activity is, from a Christian's perspective, what makes science possible: the discovery of how things work in the natural/material world is nothing other than the uncovering of how God normally does things in this physical world. But that does not prevent him, should he choose to do so, from doing something in an entirely extraordinary way—like raising Jesus from the dead. And that is one way of defining a miracle.

Practical Suggestions

The most important advice I can give for leading this discussion is not to get bogged down. The opening two chapters of Genesis raise so many disputed issues that it is easy to lose sight of the dominant theological emphases in the text. It is worth becoming

informed about some of these issues, partly so that you can deal
with them briefly and return to what is central, partly so that you
are prepared to make suggestions for further study, and partly so
that you can pursue further discussion of relatively tangential issues
with those most interested in them outside the study group itself.
But do your best to keep focused on the most central matters.

For what it is worth, in my experience most nonbelievers and
young Christians prove to be happy with the approach adopted
here. The most aggressive and sometimes probing questions come
from those who have been Christians for a longer time and who
want to get all their questions answered. There is a place for that
exercise, of course, but ideally not when the focus is on those who
are just starting out in Bible study. The more technical questions of
those who are a little more advanced can easily have the effect of
discouraging beginners from asking simpler things. So work hard
at unpacking the central themes covered in the book: who God is,
the implications for what this says about the world, what it means
to be made in the image of God, and so forth.

2

The God Who Does Not Wipe Out Rebels

Discussion Questions

1. Why is it important to notice that the serpent in Genesis 3 is not equivalent to God, a sort of mirror image bad god, but a creature who himself has rebelled against God?
2. In Genesis 3, what makes the initial question that the serpent asks Eve so disgusting, so essentially evil?
3. What elements in Genesis 3 show just how tragic and awful eating the forbidden fruit was?
4. How, in Genesis 3, does human defiance of God end up in broken human relationships?
5. Why is Genesis 3:15 sometimes called the "protevangelium," the first announcement of the gospel (that is, the "Good News" about Jesus)?
6. Why, in the Bible, is idolatry the supreme evil?
7. In the section on the curse pronounced on Adam, the book states, "The whole created order of which we are a part is

now not working properly. It is under a curse, subjected by God himself to death and decay." What is the contemporary evidence of this point?

8. According to the Bible, what do we human beings most need? What do you most need?

Suggestions for Further Reading

Perhaps the most insightful book on sin is that of Cornelius Plantinga Jr., *Not the Way It's Supposed to Be: A Breviary of Sin*, which Plantinga recently updated and condensed as a twenty-three-page essay.[1] Three other insightful books on the origin and nature of sin are Phillip D. Jensen, *Prodigal World: How We Abandoned God and Suffered the Consequences*; Pete Lowman, *A Long Way East of Eden: Could God Explain the Mess We're In?*; and Timothy Keller, *Counterfeit Gods: The Empty Promises of Money, Sex, and Power, and the Only Hope That Matters*. For theologically more advanced readers, there is Henri Blocher, *Original Sin: Illuminating the Riddle*. For an academic survey of how sin has been viewed across the centuries, consult Gary A. Anderson, *Sin: A History*, and Alan Jacobs, *Original Sin: A Cultural History*.

Inevitably, anyone wrestling with questions about the origin and nature of sin must sooner or later ponder how sin ties in to questions of human origins. Blocher's book mentioned above tackles some of those questions from a theological perspective. More accessible, and well worth reading, are two further books: Cornelius G. Hunter, *Darwin's God: Evolution and the Problem of Evil*, and especially Christian Smith, *Moral, Believing Animals: Human Personhood and Culture*.

For the way to think about sin under the framework of God's sovereignty, see John Piper, *Spectacular Sins and Their Global Purpose in the Glory of Christ*.

Two essays must be mentioned. Lest anyone think that what the Bible says about sin is disappointingly abstract prudery, see David

Starling, "The Very Practical Doctrine of Total Depravity."[2] In the chapter of *The God Who Is There* that corresponds to this one, I mention sociobiology. The best place to get caught up on the subject, in brief compass, is Kirsten Birkett, "Sociobiology and the Search for Explanation."[3]

Broader Theological and Pastoral Reflections

The subject of sin has so many facets that a very long essay would do no more than survey the field. Among the crucial points to hold in mind, however, for the sake of the cohesion of this survey of the Bible, are these:

One, the entire drama of the Bible's storyline turns on understanding how abominable sin is and what must be done to end it. All the later material on law, covenants, sacrifice, rising and falling nations, the promise of a Messiah, all the Bible says of Jesus, all the individual stories of men and women of faith or of anarchy, the anticipation of the new heaven and the new earth—every bit of it is a subset of this sweeping cosmic drama of human sin and its effects and of God addressing it.

Two, in the bibliographical section I mention the important book by Cornelius Plantinga, *Not the Way It's Supposed to Be*. Plantinga ably reflects on many aspects of sin, but one of his theses is that sin is anything against God's *shalom*—against the peace, good order, well-being, human flourishing, and integrity that were part of God's design for the created order. That is true, of course, but Plantinga himself points out that whatever stands against God's *shalom* stands against God himself. In other words, what makes sin so heinous is not that it flies in the face of some abstract moral order divorced from God but that it flies in the face of God himself and of all he has ordered. What makes sin so irreparably ugly and guilt-streaked is that it defies God.

The name for such defiance, of course, is idolatry. That is where Timothy Keller's little book *Counterfeit Gods* is so helpful: it compels us to think more comprehensively about idolatry. This analysis is so much more penetrating than the scathing, sneering (and quite mistaken) comments of Sam Harris: "Your principal concern appears to be that the Creator of the universe will take offence at something people do while naked. This prudery of yours contributes daily to the surplus of human misery."[4]

Three, at the same time, sin rapidly becomes so complex—casting its web into social relationships, community dynamics, national rivalries, oppressive ideologies, corrupted marriages, and so much more—that any human being is simultaneously guilty of sin and a victim of the sins of others, simultaneously a perpetrator and a victim, simultaneously a guilty party and a shamed fool. To begin to see how these dynamics are already grounded in the account of Genesis 3 is to begin to see what the Bible addresses; it is to begin to see that if God is the offended party, he is also our only hope.

Practical Suggestions

One, the more complex a topic and the more tentacles it has, the more important it becomes to focus on what is central to the text. Keep steering the discussion to what the text actually says!

Two, one of the hardest things to get across in many cultures today is the biblical understanding of sin. The reasons vary from culture to culture. For instance, in some languages there is no difference between "sin" and "crime," so when Christians say, "All people are sinners," they are heard to be saying, "All people are criminals"—and of course, that elicits immediate protests. Christians are left with saying something like "All people are criminals insofar as they have broken God's laws, rather than the laws of the nation."

More commonly in the Western world, "law" is often understood to be arbitrary, the product of a congress or a parliament, without any transcendent or moral standing. To think of sin, in the first place, as breaking God's law seems, to those reared in today's environment, to make sin out to be unfair, arbitrary, even manipulative. Sin is determined sociologically, so different social groupings have different sins. "All people are sinners" is merely the culturally shaped conclusion of people who think of sin in a socially determined but arbitrary way.

By contrast, here in Genesis 3, although Adam and Eve break a prohibition (the prohibition against eating the fruit of a specific tree), the sin that is described is much more complicated: it is idolatry, the erecting of counterfeit gods to displace the God who is there. The concept of idolatry is much easier for many to understand; it evokes images of betrayal, a broken relationship, the ugliness of selfish choices while spitting in the face of the wise and good Creator. In Romans 5, Paul himself recognizes that sin "reigned" from Adam to Moses, that is, from the fall to the giving of the law, which means idolatry has a certain kind of precedence over law-breaking. It is important that the substance of this chapter be well grasped before pressing on to chapter 4 and the place and function of the law.

A young schoolteacher in Northern Ireland once told me how she taught the substance of these early chapters of Genesis. Fresh out of college, she found herself a job teaching "religious education" (still common in the United Kingdom) to young boys in a rather rough school. She was making no headway at all. She decided to try another approach. Using plaster of Paris, she got them to create their own little creatures (one imagines that some of them were pretty grotesque) and then, over the next days, their own world, complete with a village, animals, a little lake, fences, and so forth. She had the boys make up the "backstory" behind each little creature and begin to weave the accounts together. Eventually she asked them to pool ideas for some rules or laws that they thought they should impose to preserve some order. The boys came up with quite a number, including a prohibition against going too close to the edge of the "world" lest they fall off and break, and a prohibition against going into the lake, where of course they would dissolve.

These and other "laws" were grouped together to see if they could
be boiled down for simplicity. The boys decided that the one law
"Do what I tell you" was the most comprehensive.

The next day, the teacher came into class and asked them to
imagine that one of the little creatures the boys had created stood
up and said to his maker, rather defiantly, "Leave me alone. This is
my world, not yours. I'll do what I want. I certainly do *not* want
you telling me what to do. Get out of here and leave me alone!"
How, then, should the boys respond?

There was a moment of stunned silence, and then one of the
boys volunteered, "I'd break his bloody legs!"

That is how the teacher introduced Genesis 3. And of course,
the degree of culpable betrayal and defiance that we human beings
display against the perfectly good, wise, and sovereign Creator is
infinitely greater.

Three, clearly it will be helpful if each participant begins to see
the nature of his or her own guilt. The issue is more than breaking a rule or a law (though it is not less than that); it is defying
our Creator, a thankless "I'll do it my way" that simultaneously
impoverishes us while attempting to diminish him. It is both stupid and wicked. We belong to a race, God's own image-bearers,
where we gravitate to such stupidity and wickedness "naturally,"
so naturally that it takes the light of Scripture to help us see how
blind we are.

The God Who Writes His Own Agreements

Discussion Questions

1. If God is like any of the three models talked about—the super-soft grandfather, the deist's God, or the mutual back-scratching God—how does each of these three understandings of God shape the way we will respond to him?
2. From what we have seen so far, how, according to the Bible, does the God who is there differ from these models?
3. If we have nothing with which we can barter with God, on what basis must any relationship with God be established?
4. What promises does God graciously give to Abraham?
5. How is the covenant God establishes between himself and Abraham ratified or sealed or established?
6. What significance do you find in Genesis 22?
7. This last question is for those who have already been exposed to a fair bit of the Bible and history: How do the promises God makes to Abraham (see question 4, above) work out in

history? In other words, how does God keep these promises?
Of what relevance are they to us today?

Suggestions for Further Reading

If you do not have time to read an entire book, this is a topic where
you can benefit enormously by reading entries in a good Bible
dictionary. Read, for instance, the entry on "covenant" in *New
Bible Dictionary*. A helpful introduction is the essay by David
Gibson, "The God of Promise: Christian Scripture as Covenantal
Relations," which is available online.[1]

A readable short volume that introduces classic covenant theology
is the work by Michael S. Horton, *God of Promise: Introducing
Covenant Theology*. The same author has penned a much longer
and more complete volume on the same subject under the title
Covenant and Eschatology: The Divine Drama. One of the best
introductions to the place of covenant in the Bible, examined in
the light of biblical theology, is the book by Paul R. Williamson,
Sealed with an Oath: Covenant in God's Unfolding Purpose.

Broader Theological and Pastoral Reflections

A great deal of discussion has taken place about what is the central
or controlling theme that holds the entire Bible together. For example, some say it is the theme of promise and fulfillment; others
say it is the theme of covenant, and so they track out the various
covenants the Bible introduces, culminating in the new covenant
that Jesus inaugurates with his own death (see Luke 22:20).

It is doubtful that such a discussion is useful for our purposes.
It is more helpful to show how the Bible uses a variety of ways to
talk about the relationship between God and his image-bearers,
and even to show how some of them are related to one another.
For example, Genesis 1 discloses God as the Creator, while we are
the creatures; implicitly, Genesis shows God to be the Judge, while

we are the idolaters—but even there, God is holding out the possibility of meeting us in our need with the promise of a seed that will crush the serpent's head. So even while God is Judge, he is the God of promise. In this chapter of the book, we have focused on God as the God of the covenant, but the covenant with Abraham embraces a variety of promises that point forward to fulfillments and ultimately to a new covenant. Later on we shall see God speaking of himself as our Father and of us as his children.

The wonderful truth of the matter is that the biblical themes are so intertwined that it is possible to move from any one of them to all the others. Those who lead these Bible studies will want to keep alert to these sorts of connections as the Bible's storyline unfolds. In other words, you can carefully observe how biblical themes intertwine, without having to make judgment calls about which themes are most important, without having to pronounce which themes constitute the "center" of the Bible. The sole exception is found in those passages where the Bible itself declares what is most important (such as 1 Cor. 15:3). There all Christians will gladly assent.

Practical Suggestions

The theme that binds together the various chapters of Genesis surveyed in this chapter is the goodness and initiative of God in dealing with his rebellious image-bearers. He calls Abraham, initiates a relationship with him, provides him with spectacular promises that propel the story forward, and then, in two dramatic steps, shows that *he himself* will somehow take on the responsibility for maintaining this covenant, for providing the needed sacrifice (see Genesis 15 and 22). The character of God, unveiled in his covenant, his promises, and his provision of sacrifice, draws us into himself. He remains our Creator (see Genesis 1) and our Judge (see Genesis 3), but he provides for his self-absorbed image-bearers a hope that is grounded in his own goodness.

4

The God Who Legislates

Discussion Questions

1. Is it possible to have absolutely no absolutes? Defend your view.
2. Where do our expressions "Old Testament" and "New Testament" (that is, the primary divisions of the Bible) come from?
3. God says that he is a jealous God. What does he mean?
4. Why does God forbid people from making an image of him?
5. Why is it significant that, according to Leviticus 16, God requires a sacrifice before anyone can enter his presence in the Most Holy Place?
6. According to Exodus 32–34, does God forgive sin or punish the guilty? If both, how can these twin stances ever be reconciled?

7. In what ways does the law of Moses point forward to Jesus?

Suggestions for Further Reading

Hundreds of books and articles have been written on law in the Bible during the last quarter century, and of course many more over the last two millennia. How Christians relate to the law is part of that discussion. For a useful survey of at least some of the major options, see the book edited by Wayne G. Strickland, *The Law, the Gospel, and the Modern Christian: Five Views*.

As indicated at the beginning of the chapter in the textbook and in the "Practical Suggestions" for chapter 2 found in this book, there is a fair bit of feeling in Western culture that law is nothing more than a social construct and no one, not even God, has the right to lay down absolutes. These are merely the reflections of power, coercive or otherwise, and should be repudiated or ignored by free people. Taken to the extreme, the name of that game is relativism. Inevitably, the robust defense of relativism turns out to be extraordinarily authoritarian. The book by James Davidson Hunter, *The Death of Character: Moral Education in an Age without Good or Evil*, persuasively argues that most Americans are losing the vocabulary necessary to talk about normative, universal, objective morality. Hunter, a Christian sociologist at the University of Virginia, shows how our school systems have systematically eliminated the vocabulary and other conditions that make character, classically understood, possible. In other words, once we have undermined notions of right and wrong grounded in normative truth, "true" moral standards dissolve, with the result that character formation degenerates to nothing more than taste or preference. One of the better popular challenges to relativism is Francis J. Beckwith and Gregory Koukl, *Relativism: Feet Firmly Planted in Mid-Air*. A probing analysis of the declining place of moral law in Western culture is a book frequently overlooked: Harold O. J. Brown, *The Sensate Culture.*

Broader Theological and Pastoral Reflections

Many theological avenues could usefully be explored: how to read a book like Leviticus, for instance, and why the Ten Commandments includes such a strong prohibition against making images of God. Many excellent contributions have probed exactly how the Old Testament sacrificial system works.[1]

But it may be enough to reflect a little on sacrifice. Many a contemporary reader feels more than a little alienated from a religious system that depends on the slaughter of animals for its most sacred rites. Even apart from the blood and gore, why is *sacrifice* so central under the law of God given by Moses?

Nevertheless, there are many facets of contemporary culture where people readily understand and even admire sacrifice. White blood corpuscles surround a dangerous alien and give their life to destroy it. A marine jumps on a live hand grenade to absorb the blast himself and thereby save the lives of his fellow soldiers. For this sacrifice he may receive the Congressional Medal of Honor. A mother bird jumps into the path between her fledgling and an approaching snake, risking and perhaps losing her life. A pedestrian runs toward a toddler who is about to be hit by a speeding truck and manages to throw the child to safety before he himself is hit and killed. We readily hold up these and other sacrifices—why should we think that God is less good or less interested in sacrifice?

The complicating factor, of course, is that the danger in these examples comes from outside the sacrificing agent, but with God it is a little different. The invading body is differentiated from the white corpuscle; the grenade has been tossed in by an enemy; the snake is quite independent of the bird; the truck cannot be confused in any way with the pedestrian. But when Old Testament sacrifices that God himself has prescribed are offered, their purpose, among others, is to avert the just wrath of God. In other words, where sin has triumphed, the greatest threat of judgment comes from God himself, for he has pronounced death on those who sin—yet God is the one who prescribes what sacrifices may avert that righteous wrath. In a way quite different from the other examples of sacrifice I just listed, God is as intimately tied to the danger people face as to the sacrificial solution that spares them. That reality will only become clearer when we study Jesus and his cross.

Practical Suggestions

One cannot too strongly stress how many young people today do *not* feel any guilt or shame for conduct that would have made their grandparents cringe. We cannot say that this is because they are more wicked or less wicked: surely we are unqualified to make such pronouncements. Rather, it is because the very categories of (absolute) right and wrong, of morality tied to law that commands and prohibits, have been questioned at deep levels. Those who hold to such categories are easily mocked: the "Church Lady" on *Saturday Night Live* was good for some laughs, with her sneering, self-righteous condescension.

As we have seen, the Bible itself explores rebellion against and alienation from our Creator-God before it explores law at great length. That sequence not only is good biblical theology (and a point that Paul picks up in Romans 5) but also turns out to be a wise approach to a generation that is generally suspicious of law. This does not mean we can duck the category of law, of course: law plays a huge role in the Bible, and one cannot even begin to understand, say, Pauline distinctions between gospel and law if one does not think through what law is, how it is related to God, how it functions within Scripture, and so forth.

At the same time, a constant effort to uphold the importance of law may have a harmful effect if it is not simultaneously tied to the grace of God in the gospel. As people begin to glimpse the truth that a purely lawless world generates the hopeless "comfort" of anarchy, as they find that they too defend at least *some* rights and wrongs (for example, how many secularists would deny that it is wrong to beat up and otherwise abuse babies?), and above all as they see that the God who is there *does* uphold distinctions between right and wrong, they may slide from suspicion of law to self-righteous legalism. As people begin to understand how biblical distinctions between right and wrong are tied to the very character of God, they may begin to think of law as good advice after all. Sadly, we want good advice more than we want good news. A steady diet of WWJD (What would Jesus do?) provides more dos and don'ts, more law. This is followed in turn by either pride or despair, depending on how well an individual thinks he or she is conforming to the prescribed pattern. But the gospel focuses less on what Jesus did, so that we may imitate him, than on what Jesus has uniquely done, so that we may trust him.

That is why it is important in this lesson not only to present a sympathetic view of the law but also to show how the law points forward beyond itself to the perfection of holiness, to the perfect sacrifice.

5

The God Who Reigns

Discussion Questions

1. What does it mean to say that God is not a constitutional monarch?
2. In the Old Testament, God is sometimes depicted as king over everything and everyone in the universe, and sometimes as king over Israel. Explain.
3. Why is a king in David's dynasty said to become God's "son" when he begins his reign?
4. During his ministry, Jesus repeatedly announces the dawning of the kingdom. When does Jesus's kingdom come?
5. What is the last enemy Jesus must overcome? How is that relevant to you?
6. Explain Oscar Cullmann's analogy about D-day and VE-day.
7. Are you in the kingdom?

Suggestions for Further Reading

An excellent introduction to the theme of the kingdom in the Old Testament is Stephen G. Dempster, *Dominion and Dynasty: A Theology of the Hebrew Bible*. A rather lengthy and overlooked (but very stimulating) volume on the kingdom in the Bible, especially as preached by Jesus, is David Seccombe, *The King of God's Kingdom*. To understand some of the current discussion from a confessional perspective, one might start with Russell D. Moore, *The Kingdom of Christ: The New Evangelical Perspective*.

Broader Theological and Pastoral Reflections

Like the theme of covenant, the theme of the kingdom can be used to organize everything in the Bible—or, better put, one can look at everything in the Bible through kingdom-colored glasses. If God makes everything, such that the existence of everything is dependent on him, then he reigns over everything. The fall (Genesis 3) can be thought of as a revolt against his reign; the rest of the Bible's storyline is nothing other than God regaining his direct reign: the end of Christ's coming is that every knee bows and acknowledges that Jesus is Lord to the glory of God (see Philippians 2).

As the book tries to make clear, the drama of God's reign, of God's kingdom, is more complicated than that. That is because in one crucial respect God's kingdom is unlike all human monarchies. God's reign operates in a mysterious providential fashion even when human beings and devils alike oppose him. His creatures cannot escape the outer boundaries of his sovereign sway. If a human king finds many of the people he rules revolting against him, regaining this kingdom means putting down the revolt and ensuring that his will holds sway. When God finds his image-bearers revolting against him, he has the power to crush the revolt entirely, but instead he continues to reign in such a way that many of his revolting image-bearers are reconciled to him, transformed, happily bowing under the lordship of Jesus. If we may speak of God "regaining" his kingdom, or of his kingdom coming, we quickly have to add that at one level God never stops reigning. God's kingdom coming in its fullness means that within the sway of his reign his will is done perfectly *without being contested*. In the new heaven and the new earth, not only will his will be done perfectly, on earth as it is in heaven, but his people will *love* to do his will and *delight* to be under the sway of him who sits on the throne and of the Lamb.

Practical Suggestions

One of the pastoral ironies is that our world is deeply suspicious of all claims to authority, while Jesus says, "All authority in heaven and on earth has been given to me" (Matt. 28:18). While the world judges that all imperialism is corrupt and that freedom presupposes the destruction of imperialism, the Bible pictures the culmination and consummation of all things as the most total imperialism that can ever be imagined. As Andrew Bain puts it, "The nub of the problem is that the gospel does in fact make imperial claims for an unassailable kingdom whose decisive victory has already been won at the cross—but whose claims remain contested in the present age until the King returns in glory to mop up those pretentious 'powers' that do not acknowledge his authority."[1]

Because such sweeping imperialism is out of favor in this anti-imperialist age, some Christians advocate playing down this theme. But that really will not do. Jesus is Lord, and in the end his subjects will universally and joyfully recognize him in the new heaven and the new earth. Those who refuse to bow to him will face the most awful and catastrophic judgment.

Yet it is essential to differentiate the imperialist sweep of God's kingdom from all other imperialisms. God really does know best; more important, his love for his image-bearers is unfathomable, extending all the way to the cross to secure their redemption. The great rulers of the imperial powers that have dotted the history of the world do not entreat alienated subjects to repent and do not then choose suffering and death in order to redeem them. Confessing the lordship of Jesus Christ becomes a joyful privilege when we ponder the love that sent this Jesus Christ to the cross on our behalf. That is the truth that must be underlined when people object to the imperialist nature of the kingdom of God.

6

The God Who Is
Unfathomably Wise

Discussion Questions

1. Why is Psalm 1 called a "wisdom psalm"?
2. Why are the absolute moral polarities found in wisdom literature so important?
3. Why does the Bible teach that it is the fool who says, "There is no God" (Ps. 14:1)?
4. "Against you only have I sinned," David says to God (see Ps. 51:4). How does this make any sense when in some way or other David has sinned against a lot of people?
5. Does the book of Job provide an answer to the question of innocent suffering?
6. Ecclesiastes warns us that we ought to live in the light of the fact that we will all give an account to God; we must all face him in the end. Is that good news or bad? What should be done about it?

7. What are some of the ways in which the parts of the Bible covered in this chapter—psalms and wisdom literature— leave us hanging, wanting to press on to clear resolutions?

Suggestions for Further Reading

During the last two decades many books have been written on the theology of the psalms, and even more on one aspect or another of wisdom literature. Only rarely do the treatments come together in one volume—and here the volume to obtain is Daniel J. Estes, *Handbook on the Wisdom Books and Psalms*. For our purposes, however, it is enough to draw attention to a little book by Peter J. Leithart, *Solomon among the Postmoderns*, and to this I turn now.

Broader Theological and Pastoral Reflections

Leithart engages with a number of postmodern thinkers by bringing his understanding of Ecclesiastes to bear on the discussion. Leithart rightly criticizes both modernity and the more recent secular postmodern thinkers who challenged modernity. He argues that the crucial domain at dispute is not epistemology (how we know things) but eschatology—the latter understood to embrace not only what happens at the end but also how we ought to live our lives in the light of the end. There is a sense in which modernity acted as if the end is already here—it looked for definitive science, definitive politics, definitive education, as if we are in the place where we can nail such things down with confidence. (This has a lot more to do with epistemology than Leithart is willing to admit, but we'll let that pass.) The postmoderns came along and argued persuasively for the indefiniteness of all interpretations. This resonates with much of the argument of Ecclesiastes: the Teacher looks at everything and concludes it is all vanity, all vaporousness. Leithart writes:

Postmodern social, technical, and cultural conditions highlight the fragility of human thought and reason, the limits of what we can know, the diversity of human language, custom, and knowledge. So does Solomon. In fact, one of Solomon's most emphatic themes in Ecclesiastes is that the world escapes our intellectual mastery as much as our technical control. Solomon pursues knowledge and wisdom, but he concludes that this pursuit too is no more than vapor and shepherding wind.[1]

The difference, however, is that the Teacher in Ecclesiastes still has an eschatology: the end of the book insists that the judgment of God finally confronts everything we are and do. The book ends by insisting that God brings all our works to judgment. While we live here now "under the sun," in this temporal space between the fall and the new heaven and the new earth, we must live our lives now under the absolute reality of final judgment to come: there is a final word that stands over all our temporary, partial, and nondefinitive words. There is a definitive interpretation after all. While the Enlightenment that characterized modernity sought for a final word and often claimed to find it, the postmodern philosopher Jacques Derrida and his friends insist that reality cannot be known (indeed, the cruder voices say there is no reality there); everything is always provisional. But Ecclesiastes says that there is an end to this provisional status of things: judgment is coming, and God will have the last say. In fact, in the light of the New Testament, the judgment has in some sense already happened; that is what the cross is about, with the result that the kingdom has been inaugurated, even while we await the consummation. Something definitive *has* already taken place in history, and *already* it changes everything.

Practical Suggestions

Today when we call to mind those thought to be wise or knowledgeable, we think of self-sufficient, mature, autonomous, perhaps self-made folk, a cut above the madding crowd. But who is wise in the Bible? Who enjoys the most admirable knowledge? The Bible insists that the fear of the Lord is the beginning of knowledge, the beginning of wisdom. One easily sees why, from the perspective of the God who is there, this must be so. For what shall it profit anyone to gain vast technical competence or political wisdom and come to the end of his or her days without being reconciled to this God? Even when it comes to knowing how to live here, in line with the mind, heart, and will of God, where does true wisdom lie? So it is not too surprising that the Bible insists that the person who says there is no God is the fool, no matter how many advanced degrees he or she has achieved. This stance is obvious once one begins with the God who is there.

In other words, the fundamental lesson that must be communicated is not so much the individual contribution of this or that psalm, or of each wisdom book (as helpful as it is to learn such material), but what true wisdom consists in. Through the experiences reflected in the psalms and the reflection found in the wisdom literature, we return once again to the most basic need: the need to know the living God.

A little over a year ago the British Humanist Association ran ads on London buses reading, "There's probably no God. Now stop worrying and enjoy your life." It is fascinating that the Association felt it wise to insert "probably"; if the person who says there is no God is a fool, I suppose this slogan represents cautious folly. But why the British Humanist Association thinks that the nonexistence of God should reduce worry is more than a little puzzling. If there is no God, it is hard to see how there is transcendent meaning. Worse, no one is in charge, so there is no assurance that justice will be served at the end; there is no one to look after me, no one I can trust. The Association seems to think that the nonexistence of God liberates us to enjoy life. That presupposes that the God of the Bible is the cosmic party pooper, whose primary glee is to make us miserable. But the Bible says that Christ brings us abundant joy and that at God's right hand are pleasures forevermore. He is the source of genuine wisdom and knowledge that continue into eternity.

These are the sorts of associations we should be seeking to establish in this study.

7

The God Who Becomes
a Human Being

Discussion Questions

1. Six centuries before Jesus was born, the prophet Jeremiah promised a new covenant. What does this promise implicitly say about the old (Mosaic) covenant?
2. What does the name "Jesus" mean? Why is that meaning important?
3. What does "Trinity" mean?
4. Where in John's prologue (John 1:1–18) does John make it clear that the "Word" is simultaneously God's own peer and God's own self?
5. What does "incarnation" mean?
6. List some of the thematic connections between John 1:14–18 on the one hand and Exodus 32–34 on the other. Taken together, what do they mean?
7. We cannot look directly on God, according to John 1:18. What is, at present, the closest we can come?

8. In what ways does Jesus most spectacularly show that he is full of grace and truth?

Suggestions for Further Reading

"Must" reading at an introductory level for understanding the way various Old Testament passages and institutions point forward to Christ is Tremper Longman III, *Immanuel in Our Place: Seeing Christ in Israel's Worship*. One should not miss Michael P. V. Barrett, *Beginning at Moses: A Guide to Finding Christ in the Old Testament*.

Perhaps the best single book on the deity of Christ, from a strictly exegetical point of view focusing on passages that use the word "God" to refer to Jesus, is that of Murray J. Harris, *Jesus as God: The New Testament Use of* Theos *in Reference to Jesus*. A more accessible book is Robert M. Bowman Jr. and J. Ed Komoszewski, *Putting Jesus in His Place: The Case for the Deity of Christ*. A thorough broad-based study of the incarnation is Millard J. Erickson, *The Word Became Flesh: A Contemporary Incarnational Christology*. Equally useful is his *God in Three Persons: A Contemporary Interpretation of the Trinity*. A fresh and important contribution is that of Richard Bauckham, *God Crucified: Monotheism and Christology in the New Testament*. Finally, a superb book on some of the historical questions surrounding Jesus, not least his uniqueness, is the fine book by James R. Edwards, *Is Jesus the Only Savior?* and two excellent essays online by Craig Blomberg and Harold A. Netland respectively.[1]

Broader Theological and Pastoral Reflections

In his 1903 book *The Dynasts*, Thomas Hardy describes God as "the dreaming, dark, dumb Thing that turns the handle of this idle show."[2] Hardy's God is not a person but a thing. It is devoid of relationships, friendship, fellowship, warmth. It is utterly silent ("dumb"); it cannot speak. Yet in some ways it controls our lives, presumably in some sort of impersonal, amoral, purposeless, and fatalistic fashion, as it "turns the handle of this idle show."

The God of the Bible, the God who is there, is not like that. Though he is sovereign, he is also personal: he is presented as passionate, relational, warm, indignant, loving, wrathful. Above all, he is the God who communicates—not only in spectacular events, and not only in nature (recall the poetry of Psalm 19:1–2: "The heavens declare the glory of God; the skies proclaim the work of his hands. Day after day they pour forth speech; night after night they display knowledge"), but also in words that have come down to us in the Bible. So important is this category of "word" that eventually it is applied to the highest and greatest revelation of all: the revelation of God in the person of his Son, who is consequently called God's Word, his self-expression. For this Word "became flesh" (John 1:14). Jesus is not merely a spokesperson for God, a kind of souped-up prophet; he is the explanation of God, the narrative of God, the exegesis of God. The same argument, in slightly different words, is found in Hebrews 1:1–4.

In other words, while pondering the incarnation or wrestling with the doctrine of the Trinity, one must see that a huge claim to *revelation* is being made—the revelation of God. If this is taken seriously, one can never again reduce Christianity to the level of mere ritual and popular religion: it is bound up with God becoming a man, with revelation of the most exquisitely high order. Jesus cannot be reduced to the level of guru equivalent to other gurus. He is utterly unique.

Practical Suggestions

As important as the content of this chapter is—tracing some of the patterns of messianic expectation, the nature of the incarnation— the *way* one talks about the material in group discussion is no less important. The truth of who Jesus Christ is must never be served up cold—especially not to people who are inquiring about the Christian faith and to young believers. Choose words and attitudes well, both for your own spiritual well-being and for the well-being of those you are teaching. Christ as God and man must evoke awe, reverence, worship, and wonder.

Those who have studied theology may happily speak of Christology and suffuse the word with adoration, but for beginners the word will have such associations only if the person leading the discussion establishes the link between confession and adoration by his or her own attitude.

8

The God Who Grants New Birth

Discussion Questions

1. Granted the human dilemma depicted in the Bible's storyline, what three things do we human beings need?
2. What does "new birth" or "born again" terminology conjure up in our world? What does it conjure up in Jesus's mind?
3. What is the difference in the flow of logic between Barna and the Bible, so far as the new birth is concerned?
4. What does "born of water and the Spirit" (John 3:5) mean?
5. According to John 3, why could Jesus speak with such knowledge and authority about the new birth?
6. What are the connections between this account of the new birth in John 3 and the Old Testament account of the bronze serpent in Numbers 21?
7. Have you been born again?

Suggestions for Further Reading

The best short book on the new birth in recent times is John Piper, *Finally Alive: What Happens When We Are Born Again*. It is pitched at a level such that you could give it to almost anyone. A theological treatment is found in Helmut Burkhardt, *The Biblical Doctrine of Regeneration*. Those interested in richer (though slightly older) fare might read the relevant sections of Herman Bavinck, *Reformed Dogmatics*, volume 4: *Holy Spirit, Church, and New Creation*. Speaking of the new creation, the links between new birth and new creation are many, so that probing along the theme of new creation (especially in Pauline studies) brings up many useful and thought-provoking parallels.

Finally, because the new birth theme is treated at length in only a handful of New Testament passages (though it is alluded to many more times), in this case careful commentary work on a few passages (not only John 3:1–21 but also, say, 1 Peter 1:23–25) will pay dividends in understanding.

Broader Theological and Pastoral Reflections

Owing to the fact that the doctrine of justification has been challenged in some influential circles during the past three decades, evangelical Christians have devoted more attention to this topic than to many others. We have held conferences on the subject, written books, engaged in debates, reminded ourselves that for the Reformers justification is the doctrine by which the church stands or falls, and so forth. Such responses were needed; in God's providence, they were beneficial, for unless something is challenged, we have a tendency to become sloppy in our thinking and lacking in depth, precision, and biblical faithfulness.

No Christian, however, would say that justification is the only doctrine important to what the Bible says about salvation. One could even make a case that those elements that are *not* being disputed are the ones most subject to *unwitting* distortion. There have been times when Christians spoke most urgently about the necessity of being born again, partly to distinguish real, vital Christianity from its anemic cousin, merely cultural Christianity. As the chapter in *The God Who Is There* suggests, many secularists consider "born-again Christians" to be the more fanatical variety, while in some culturally conservative parts of the country just about everyone and his cousin uses the same expression for useful self-designation, even where there is no appreciable difference in values or outlook from others in the community who do not think of themselves as Christians at all.

The fundamental complementary relationship established by emphasizing *both* justification *and* regeneration ("new birth") is the wholeness intrinsic to talking about *both* our standing with God *and* the beginning of such powerful life from God that our lives are observably changed. Of course, behavior modification can be achieved by many different techniques, so behavior modification *without* being reconciled to God, declared just before him, is scarcely adequate. But those who rest comfortably in justification but whose conduct is indistinguishable from that of the world, the flesh, and the devil call into question that status with God because no one is truly justified who is not also regenerate: you cannot have one without the other.

Of course, there are other dimensions to salvation—dimensions tied to our relationships with others and what it means to be the body of Christ (ecclesiology), dimensions tied to the final consummation and resurrection existence in the new heaven and the new earth and the way this reality feeds back into our own place and time (eschatology), dimensions bound up with the way Christians grow in grace (traditionally called sanctification), and more. Some of these will be lightly explored in later chapters (especially chapter 12). What is important is the holistic nature of what the Bible says about salvation. Failure to grasp at least some of the ways these dimensions hold together invariably ushers in a truncated understanding of what the God who is there has done to redeem us back to himself, and thus also a truncated Christian experience.

Many theologians, not least in the Dutch Reformed tradition, insist that people receive both justification and sanctification by faith alone, but they are not always explicit about why or how this is the case. By contrast, Jonathan Edwards asserts that a high percentage of all virtue is common virtue, i.e., the fruit of common grace. These must be distinguished from gospel grace and gospel virtue. Two motives commonly lie behind common virtue: fear and pride. The fear may be of God, law, parents, what others might think, and more; the pride says, in effect, "I am not as others are." Individuals who learn not to commit adultery or not to lie refrain from adultery and lying not because of a transformed heart but because of fear and pride. They do not commit adultery and do not lie, not because they love sexual purity and truth-telling, or for God's sake, but for their own sake. They do not have transformed hearts and minds but restrained hearts and minds. The irony is that a person may lie and even commit adultery out of fear and pride—and another may refuse to lie and commit adultery equally out of pride. In short, the line between committing explicit sins and the works-righteousness of not committing those sins is very thin: both common vices and common virtues may be nourished by fear and pride. To preach and teach mere morality may actually strengthen fear and pride within the congregations of the living God. But where the gospel takes hold of people, where both justification and regeneration have taken place, we understand that we have been accepted and remain accepted out of sheer grace, we receive this by faith, and our ethics springs out of gratitude for this grace.

As Charlotte Brontë wrote in *Jane Eyre*, "Conventionality is not morality. Self-righteousness is not religion. To attack the first is not to assail the last. To pluck the mask from the face of the Pharisee, is not to lift an impious hand to the Crown of Thorns."[1]

Practical Suggestions

Four emphases will prove helpful:

One, ensure that the participants understand how both justification and regeneration address the threefold dilemma that all human
beings have to face this side of the fall (outlined at the beginning
of this chapter in the book).

Two, work at making clear how what we know about new birth
springs from revelation—from who Jesus is and where he came
from. To teach such material so authoritatively turns, in John's
Gospel, on the reality of the incarnation—and thus chapter 7 of
The God Who Is There grounds chapter 8.

Three, show how new birth (i.e., regeneration) turns on Jesus
being "lifted up" on the cross.

Four, try to make clear, both from the material in the textbook
and with the help of the further theological and pastoral reflections (see above), the nature of the changed life. The change is first
and foremost internal and in attitude as the believer acknowledges
his or her sheer indebtedness to grace. For those with antisocial
habits of life, the external changes brought about by being born
again will be observable and profound; for those trained in con-
ventional morality, superficial observers may not initially detect a
huge change, but the transformation of the heart brought about by
the new birth changes how and why things are done or not done,
and it cannot finally be suppressed.

The God Who Loves

Discussion Questions

1. How should we distinguish being morally discerning from being judgmental?
2. List five ways the Bible speaks about the love of God.
3. Does God love everyone exactly the same?
4. In the text "God so loved the world," what is the meaning of "world" that makes God's love so wonderfully admirable?
5. What is meant by the claim that the measure of God's love for us is Jesus?
6. What is the *purpose* of God giving us his Son?
7. How does the love of God for us rightly stir gladness and gratitude within us?

Suggestions for Further Reading

Although there are many excellent books on the theme of God's love as found in particular biblical books or passages (e.g., in John's

Gospel, the Sermon on the Mount, Hosea, and so forth), there are far fewer good books (if one ignores the merely sentimental contributions) on the love of God as a great theological theme in all of Scripture.

There are three ways of circumventing this deficiency. First, select a handful of biblical passages that forcefully express the theme of the love of God (e.g., the book of Hosea, especially chapter 11; John 3:16–17; Gal. 2:20; 1 John 4:7–10) and study what the best commentaries and theologies say about such passages. Among the passages that helpfully disclose some of the dimensions of God's love is the parable of the lost sons (Luke 15:11–32). Two books are particularly helpful in studying this passage: Kenneth E. Bailey, *Finding the Lost: Cultural Keys to Luke 15*, and, at a more popular level, Timothy Keller, *The Prodigal God: Recovering the Heart of the Christian Faith*.

Second, many of the better treatments of passages that talk about *our love for God or for others* (as opposed to *his love for us*) carefully show how our love for God and others is at best a pale imitation of his love for us. For instance, 1 Corinthians 13, the so-called "love chapter," is clearly talking about *Christian* love, yet a classic book like Jonathan Edwards's *Charity and Its Fruits* introduces us as well to *God's* love.

Third, the best devotional books on the gospel meditate on how the cross of Christ displays God's love. A recent example is Milton Vincent, *A Gospel Primer for Christians: Learning to See the Glories of God's Love*. (See also the recommended reading in the next two chapters.)

I have written two short books on the topic: *The Difficult Doctrine of the Love of God* and *Love in Hard Places*. The first outlines various ways the Bible talks about the love of God and teases out some theological and pastoral implications. The second outlines various ways the Bible speaks of Christian love and attempts to tie these ways to God's love as well.

Broader Theological and Pastoral Reflections

I just mentioned the parable of the prodigal sons (and the respective works of Kenneth Bailey and Timothy Keller). Sometimes a parable becomes so superficially familiar to us that we overlook the impact it would have enjoyed in the first-century culture where it was first delivered.

At every point in the story, the father, representing God, does not act as a first-century Palestinian Jewish father would. He accedes to the younger son's greedy, disrespectful, and insolent demand to be given his share of the inheritance—a demand which is a way of saying that he would prefer it if the father were dead. Wealth in those days was in land and animals. For the father to agree would mean selling part of his estate—and that would be a public shame and disgrace. This too the father bears. After squandering and dissipating his inheritance, the foolish son, now desperate, finally decides to return home. He knows he will have to eat humble pie but hopes to work for his father, earn his way, and who knows? Perhaps he will be able to pay back much of what he has burned up. But the father will have none of it. He has been looking for his son, waiting for him, and sees him a long way off. Picking up his long skirts, he runs to his son, embraces him, and kisses him. None of this is first-century oriental patriarchal behavior. And then instead of entering into some sort of negotiated truce that will enable the son to begin to repay what he has lost, the father orders a feast and insists on receiving the wanderer home as a son, not a hired hand. When the older brother pouts and whines, refusing to join in a banquet put on by his father, his insult to the old man is almost as great as that of the younger son. Once again, however, it is the father who goes out to the son (unthinkable! as unthinkable as a patriarch picking up his skirts and running!) to reason with him.

In other words, contrary to what *both* sons think, *neither* of them can sustain a relationship with their father on the basis of hard work and achievement. What the father offers outstrips their squalid and self-focused plans: he provides love, grace, forgiveness, humility welcoming the rebel home, sonship, and restoration to the family.

Similar summaries of other passages—the book of Hosea, perhaps—will go a long way toward fleshing out in thought and emotion what it means to affirm that the God who is there is the God who loves.[1]

Practical Suggestions

In addition to teaching the positive content of this chapter on the love of God, it is worth devoting a bit of time to gently overturning some of those mawkish sentimentalities about God's love that make him indistinguishable from a slightly disreputable granddad who is a bit past his "sell by" date and who thinks that he shows his love by indulgently providing for every need and greed of his unruly brood.

One of the ways to get this across is to show how God is never less than the perfection of all his attributes all the time. It is not as if he is holy some days, and other days he prefers to be loving; it is not as if he is near us in gracious self-disclosure at the beginning of the week but might drift off into distant deism by the weekend. He is God. Although he may disclose more of one attribute than another in a particular personal interaction with some of his image-bearers, he never relinquishes any of his perfections. One might usefully call to mind, for example, what God says of himself in Exodus 34:5–7 (briefly mentioned in the fourth chapter of *The God Who Is There*). Only then will we begin to see the shining glory of his love, ablaze with warmth and compassion even in the context of the perfection of his justice and holiness. Getting this balance of truths across provides the best possible preparation for the next two chapters, both of which take us to the cross.

10

The God Who Dies— and Lives Again

Discussion Questions

1. Why does the Bible keep insisting that Jesus was born in order to die?
2. What is irony?
3. What are the ironies of the cross?
4. In one sense, it is not correct to say that God died. Jesus is the one who died, not God the Father. Yet as we have seen, some New Testament texts stretch all the way to warranting the truth that in some sense, when Jesus died, God died. Why?
5. Why does Thomas doubt that Jesus has risen from the dead?
6. When Thomas sees Jesus alive on the second Sunday, he exclaims, "My Lord and my God!" Why does he say so much, instead of something smaller and weaker such as "You *are* alive!"?

7. Why is it that in the ultimate sense only God can forgive sins?

Suggestions for Further Reading

Because the cross and the resurrection of Jesus stand at the very center of the Christian faith, inevitably a huge number of books have been written about these themes. To understand some of the words connected with Jesus's death on the cross, one might usefully begin with Paul Wells, *Cross Words: The Biblical Doctrine of the Atonement*. A useful survey of quite a lot of relevant biblical passages is found in Mark Meynell, *Cross-Examined: The Life-Changing Power of the Death of Jesus*. A thoroughly penetrating treatment of the theology of the atonement is found in J. I. Packer and Mark Dever, *In My Place Condemned He Stood: Celebrating the Glory of the Atonement*. A longer treatment that interacts a little more with writers who try in one fashion or another to domesticate the cross is the volume by Steve Jeffery, Mike Ovey, and Andrew Sach, *Pierced for Our Transgressions: Rediscovering the Glory of Penal Substitution*. Then there are excellent attempts to understand how the theme of the cross is unpacked within a particular New Testament book—for example, Peter G. Bolt, *The Cross from a Distance: Atonement in Mark's Gospel*.

As for Jesus's resurrection, a book still worth giving to some people who are just beginning to read about the resurrection is a slim, older volume by Frank Morison, *Who Moved the Stone?* An updated approach is found in Gary R. Habermas and Michael R. Ligona, *The Case for the Resurrection of Jesus*. Probably the most important book on the resurrection in the last hundred years is the massive volume by N. T. Wright, *The Resurrection of the Son of God*. I have attempted to bring together a handful of themes related to both the cross and the resurrection by expounding a selection of New Testament passages in *Scandalous: The Cross and Resurrection of Jesus*.

Broader Theological and Pastoral Reflections

Because in the next chapter of *The God Who Is There* we probe the significance of the death of Jesus a little more deeply, in this section I shall instead focus on Jesus's resurrection.

It is one thing to be persuaded by the evidence of the *fact* of Jesus's resurrection; it is another to grasp a little more of its *significance*.

In the Bible, a handful of people were brought back from the dead before Jesus. One of the most notable was Lazarus, brought back from the dead by Jesus himself (see John 11). Yet Paul insists that Jesus is the *firstfruits* of the resurrection of Christ's people at the end of the age (see 1 Cor. 15:20). What makes his resurrection so special, especially if he is not, sequentially, the first? Apart from the question of *who* this Jesus is who has been resurrected—none less than the incarnate Son of God, who by his death atoned for the sins of all his people—the New Testament texts insist that his resurrection is unique. True, Lazarus was brought back to life in bodily form after spending even more time in the grave than Jesus did. But his body remained an ordinary body; presumably Lazarus died again. By contrast, after his resurrection Jesus is said to possess a "spiritual body" (1 Cor. 15:44), whatever this difficult expression means. Jesus's post-death body has some sort of continuity with his pre-death body (the marks of the wounds are still there); it is certainly a genuine *body* in the sense that Jesus could be touched and handled, and he could eat with his disciples. Yet it was more than a body as you and I know it. Jesus continues to be a human being forever, a resurrected spirit-body human being—and our resurrection bodies at the end will resemble his. Our destiny is not immaterial existence; rather, our ultimate destiny is resurrection existence (see 2 Cor. 5:1–10) in the new heaven *and the new earth*. Only Jesus has undergone this transformation to resurrection existence. He is the firstfruits of it, the one who has secured it for us.

We can scarcely imagine the power that God exercised to bring Jesus back from the dead, not least in this transformed resurrection body. But the encouraging thing is that the Bible says that the power that God exerted in raising Jesus from the dead is the very same "mighty strength" he exerts in us and for us who believe (see Eph. 1:19–20). Indeed, Paul prays for the Ephesian believers to the end that this same power may strengthen us in our inner being by God's Spirit and, further, that we might have the power, together with other Christians, to grasp how wide and long and high and deep is the love of Christ (see Eph. 3:14–19). That is why biblical Christianity can never be reduced to forensic justification (as important as that theme is): it is also the *power* of God that brings salvation to everyone who believes (see Rom. 1:16).

Practical Suggestions

If the participants in the group are largely ignorant of the biblical text (as is likely for this sort of study), it might be a good idea to break up the session with appropriate readings. These might be drawn from any of the passion narratives. It would be wise to include Isaiah 52:13–53:12. Conclude with a selection from 1 Corinthians 15. Either make the readings corporate (with the words on a screen or on a handout) or, if the passages are read by an individual, make sure that individual is an excellent reader and has practiced them in advance.

11

The God Who Declares
the Guilty Just

Discussion Questions

1. Why is it impossible to be acquitted with justice on the ground of the good things we do?
2. What is the main theme of Romans 1:18–3:20, i.e., the passage leading up to the paragraph we study in this chapter?
3. What are two or three ways in which the Old Testament anticipates or points ahead to Jesus?
4. Paul sets forth the availability of God's righteousness to all human beings without racial distinction but on the condition of faith. Why is this good news?
5. What is redemption?
6. What is propitiation?
7. Explain what Paul means when he says that in the cross God is both *just* and the one who *justifies* those who have faith in Jesus.
8. In the Bible, how is faith related to truth?

Suggestions for Further Reading

Chapter 10 focuses on Jesus's cross and resurrection; this chapter unpacks further aspects of the cross. For this reason, all the books on the cross listed under this heading in the last chapter continue to be of use here.

But I shall mention three or four more, beginning with the most accessible. John Piper's *The Passion of Jesus Christ: Fifty Reasons Why He Came to Die* is an excellent survey of important themes on the atonement, cast in a devotional style that elicits gratitude and adoration. It is worth reading Michael E. Wittmer, *Don't Stop Believing: Why Living Like Jesus Is Not Enough.* Graham Cole's *God the Peacemaker: How Atonement Brings Shalom* is especially important; it is a robust theology of the cross that establishes its points by sweeping through the entire Bible, and it deserves a place on the bookshelves of thoughtful Christians everywhere. Still worth reading for its simple clarity is John Stott, *The Cross of Christ: 20th Anniversary Edition.*

Broader Theological and Pastoral Reflections

It will be useful to reflect on two things.

First, this is the appropriate place to tie the cross to the fundamental problem that first comes to light in Genesis 3 (discussed in the second chapter of *The God Who Is There*). This is how the God who made us and who rightly stands indignant, morally outraged, at the idolatrous ingratitude of his image-bearers finally responds to their need: in the person of his Son, he bears the death sentence he himself has imposed in the holiness of his justice.

This is what theologians are talking about when they speak of "penal substitution." The word *substitution* summarizes the fact that Jesus substitutes himself for us, taking our punishment upon himself; the word *penal* reminds us that what he bears is punishment, the result of righteous judicial pronouncement.

Second, many who write and teach about the cross today speak of the various "models of the atonement" (I confess I do not like the word "models," but we'll stick with it). In this way of thinking, penal substitution is one model for understanding the cross, but there are others. For instance, the *Christus Victor* model emphasizes Jesus's victory over death, destruction, and the devil. The moral-exemplary model thinks of Jesus's sufferings on the cross as constituting a pattern for his disciples to emulate. Theologians commonly list half a dozen of these "models of the atonement," showing how prominent thinkers and movements have favored this model or that model over against others and suggesting that the choice is ours.

This is a sad error with even sadder consequences. Insofar as any of the "models" of the atonement can be shown to be in line with what Scripture says, then the obvious question is this: how do these various so-called models of the atonement, models sanctioned by Scripture, relate to each other *within Scripture*? For if they are *all* within Scripture, then Christians, living as they do under the authority of the Bible, want to embrace *all* these models. They refuse to choose just one, for implicitly that means they are walking away from *other* models that the Bible sanctions. Once again, then, the question is how these models fit together in the Bible, and therefore how they should fit together in our own thinking and theology.

I hold that the heart of all of the Bible's teaching about the cross is penal substitution. This is not only because of the enormous emphasis Scripture places on the wrath of God in the just condemnation of our sin, a wrath that is satisfied by the death of God's own chosen substitute, but also because of the way these various models relate to each other. If one begins with penal substitution, it is fairly straightforward to reason from there to all the other models; if one begins anywhere else, the same cannot be said. For instance, if one begins with the understanding of the cross unpacked in Romans 3, it is easy enough to see how the *Christus*

Victor theme follows: the Christ who is the propitiation for our sins thereby defeats death, frustrates the devil, and will bring to a final end all the savage barbarisms of this fallen and broken world: he is the Victor. Equally, it is easy enough to see how Christ's immeasurable self-denial and limitless love, displayed in the cross, constitute a formidable example for his redeemed people to imitate. But it is far more difficult to see the logic running the other way.

Although Romans 3 treats the sacrifice of Christ in legal and righteousness categories, one easily discovers that similar notions of penal substitution are often tied in the New Testament to priestly notions of access to God and mediation. No book in the New Testament is stronger in this regard than the epistle to the Hebrews, which powerfully shows how the sacrifices of the Old Testament, especially the Day of Atonement (see Leviticus 16 and chapter 4 of *The God Who Is There*), work out in terms of the new covenant.

Whether in the priestly categories of Hebrews or the legal categories of Romans, at the very heart of the meaning of the cross is one who is wounded for our transgressions, one who bears our guilt in his own body on the tree, one who died our death that we might live.

Practical Suggestions

I have found it helpful, in the course of unpacking what the Bible says about the cross, to quietly read out loud or sing a number of hymns about the cross. Large numbers of excellent examples easily come to mind: "And Can It Be"; "I Saw One Hanging on a Tree"; "Alas, and Did My Savior Bleed"; "O Sacred Head, Now Wounded"; "Before the Throne of God Above"; "The Power of the Cross"; "How Deep the Father's Love for Us." Those who know Christian hymnody will recognize that these have been pulled from a thousand-year span. The point, however, is that there is something impoverished about explaining the cross without contrition and adoration.

12

The God Who Gathers and Transforms His People

Discussion Questions

1. Why is the scale of Christian commitment, measured from nominalism to fanaticism, a mischievous scale?
2. According to Ephesians 2:8–10, what is the *purpose* of being saved by grace through faith?
3. Is it possible to be a biblically faithful Christian and separate oneself entirely from a local church?
4. We observed that one fundamental Christian motivation of great importance is not so much an abstract desire for obedience as gratitude for what God has done for us in Christ. How is this way of looking at things utterly transforming?
5. Why is greed labeled idolatry?
6. The chapter being reviewed notes a number of New Testament passages that depict suffering because one is a Christian as a privilege, as a sign of grace. How can this be? How will such suffering transform our attitudes?

7. What do we learn from the reflection of John Newton, written toward the end of his life and cited in this chapter?

Suggestions for Further Reading

A fine example of how to respond to those who say Christianity's heritage is nothing but pride and strife is the fine volume by Vincent Carroll and David Shiflett, *Christianity on Trial: Arguments against Anti-Religious Bigotry.*

The textbook devotes a little time in this chapter to the church. In an age when many claim they want to embrace Christ but frankly have no time for the church, it is more than a little refreshing to read Kevin DeYoung and Ted Kluck, *Why We Love the Church: In Praise of Institutions and Organized Religion.* A helpful recent book on the church is by Jonathan Leeman, *The Church and the Surprising Offense of God's Love: Reintroducing the Doctrines of Church Membership and Discipline.* Very important is Mark Dever, *Nine Marks of a Healthy Church.* Perhaps I should also mention my little book *The Cross and Christian Ministry: Leadership Lessons from 1 Corinthians.*

Broader Theological and Pastoral Reflections

The themes of this chapter serve to tie together a number of disparate pieces. Without using the terminology of regeneration or "new birth" (see chapter 8 of the textbook), the cited New Testament passages overflow with transformational language: empowered by the Spirit, Christians become God-centered. They learn to forgive one another because they know they have been forgiven; they know that God accepts them freely because of what Christ has borne for them, so they strive less to be accepted (and so far as they succeed in this regard, they escape the twin chains of pride and fear) and become more eager to accept others.

We earlier noted that the fall brought about guilt before God, contaminated lives, disruption in every relationship, and the degeneration of the created order. As justification addresses our guilt before God, so God's power in transforming us both ensures we distance ourselves from our sins and self-focus and rebuilds us in part through the dynamic of the transformed relationships that are ours within the church, the congregation of the people of God.

This chapter mentions baptism only briefly. Here, however, would be a good place to introduce baptism and the Lord's Supper to participants in the study.

Practical Suggestions

The material in this chapter is hugely enjoyable to teach. The range of possible passages to pick up is great. One might, for instance, read together the love chapter, 1 Corinthians 13, or survey Revelation 12, depending on the skill of the leader.

The crucial focus, however, is to avoid teaching transformative behavior as if it were brought about by little more than a lengthy list of "Do this" prescriptions and "Don't do that" prohibitions. That is what far too many people think Christianity is about. That may reflect many religions: the endless duties establish distinct patterns of religious behavior. But it does a huge injustice to any fair treatment of the gospel. So in tackling the various virtues held up by the biblical texts cited in this chapter, it is important to show how they spring from the gospel itself, how gratitude that has been nurtured in grace generates them, how a Spirit-impelled desire to imitate Jesus is part of rudimentary Christian confession.

13

The God
Who Is Very Angry

Discussion Questions

1. Why does talk about the wrath of God tend to make us uncomfortable?
2. What is "the eternal gospel" in Revelation 14:6–7?
3. How does Revelation 4–5 unpack for us what the gospel is?
4. What do each of the two agricultural metaphors found in Revelation 14:14–20 teach us about the final judgment?
5. Many have charged that talking about hell is manipulative. When might such talk be manipulative, and when is it not manipulative?
6. Why should we insist that when Christians teach and preach about hell, they should do so with tears and not with self-righteous rage?

Suggestions for Further Reading

Even some Christians have tried to displace hell with something less eternal—annihilationism, for example. One of the better responses is that of Robert A. Peterson, *Hell on Trial: The Case for Eternal Punishment*. More useful, perhaps, is the volume edited by Christopher Morgan and Robert A. Peterson, *Hell under Fire: Modern Scholarship Reinvents Eternal Punishment*. I have briefly addressed the subject in one chapter of *The Gagging of God*.

Broader Theological and Pastoral Reflections

Doubtless many think that hell, if it exists, is for really bad people, like the guards at Auschwitz, perhaps. What this overlooks is that the guards at Auschwitz were just ordinary people from a sophisticated and highly educated culture. A number of photographs have come to light showing these guards, including prominent leaders such as Rudolf Hoess and the infamous Josef Mengele (who performed cruel medical experiments on camp inmates) at Solahütte, a retreat center for SS personnel located a mere 30 kilometers from Auschwitz. These photographs disclose merry times—eating berries, mugging for the camera, lighting a Christmas tree. One is thus introduced to what Hannah Arendt famously called "the banality of evil": one of the most revolting elements of the evil was the sheer thoughtlessness of it all. Yet although this is an evil of a high order, from a biblical perspective the ugliest evil, the highest order of evil, is the erection of idols, the failure to love God with heart and soul and mind and strength. We may console ourselves with self-deceptive comfort that our culture would never act like that of Nazi Germany, but a little self-knowledge enables us to imagine descending to similar levels, while reflection on the biblical themes shows that these levels are merely symptoms of a far deeper corruption that, in its idolatrous independence, has happily and mockingly ignored the God who is there and thereby attracted his wrath.

There is some truth to the view that hell is the culmination of what we have become, of what we have made of ourselves. Romans 1 talks repeatedly of God giving us over to the passions of our own hearts. Part of the judgment that falls on us, then, is nothing other than God giving us over to the most sinful beings we most want to become. Yet the Bible also speaks of hell as the outworking of God's judgment upon us. It is not that God is distantly watching us make a mess of things while he wrings his hands and wishes he could do more to help us. Rather, in the end God's wrath is meted out. That is why the gospel urges us to be reconciled to this God before it is too late. Salvation turns on finding our refuge in him.

Hell reminds us of our utter dependence on God. It was willful *independence* that lay at the heart of the fall (see Genesis 3). But tossing away our dependence on the Creator God who made us is equivalent to tossing away our life: death follows. When we have no experience of the grace that saves and redeems and transforms God's people, and when we lose the providential support that maintains us in this broken world, the result is hell.

Practical Suggestions

Never make jokes about hell. They are in worse taste than jokes about Auschwitz.

Wise teachers of Scripture who are working through passages on judgment and hell will avoid two common stances. The *first* is morally supercilious, talking about what *they* deserve, without any awareness that it is what we *all* deserve apart from the grace of God. The *second* keeps repeating that the theme is repugnant, but faithfulness to Scripture demands that the passage be taught anyway. This latter stance is self-promoting. It sounds as if I am saying, "I resolve to be faithful to Scripture, although, quite frankly,

I dislike what it is saying" (implying, of course, that my moral sensibilities are superior to God's!). One must work toward having the deepest shared sympathy with God's perspective about hell, as about everything else.

And always warn people to flee from the wrath to come.

14

The God Who Triumphs

Discussion Questions

1. The words quoted at the beginning of the chapter, "For where your treasure is, there your heart will be also" are found in the Sermon on the Mount (Matt. 6:21). What do they mean?
2. Why is the new Jerusalem built like a cube?
3. Revelation 21:4 describes the new Jerusalem in terms of negation, i.e., in terms of what will not be allowed to exist there. Why is it easier to describe the new Jerusalem in terms of negation than in positive description?
4. What is missing from the new Jerusalem? Why?
5. What is described here as the *very best* feature of the new Jerusalem?
6. What does it mean to live now in the light of the new heaven and the new earth?
7. Are you ready for the new heaven and the new earth?

Suggestions for Further Reading

A useful introductory book is that of Bruce Milne, *The Message of Heaven and Hell*. A helpful summary of Jonathan Edwards's complex thought on the subject is Owen Strachan and Douglas Sweeney, *Jonathan Edwards on Heaven and Hell*. Once again it is useful to make a list of prospective passages that focus on the subject and to read good commentaries and other useful material on the passages in question—for example, Isaiah 11.

Broader Theological and Pastoral Reflections

I know of classes in introductory biblical theology in which, for the first assignment, the lecturer requires that students write an essay on Revelation 21–22 and briefly trace out from these two chapters all the material that has Old Testament roots. Obviously an advanced student could easily get a PhD or two out of that assignment, not least because many of the connections are allusive and subtle. Yet the point needs to be made both for students who are just setting out and for students who have been studying the Bible for a long time: these two chapters are the climax not only of the book of Revelation but also of the whole Bible.

The "new heaven and the new earth" language calls to mind not only the original creation of Genesis 1 but the promise of renovation (see Isa. 66:22). Jerusalem is not only the ancient city in the Middle East but the promise of utopia. It casts a social vision of spirituality: a city is the place where many people live and work and serve. It is the city of the Davidic king, the place of the temple—only now the entire city has become the Most Holy Place of the temple. This Davidic king is also the sacrificial lamb of Revelation 5, which shows that he emerges from the very throne of God, bringing to mind wonderful elements of Christology as well as the supreme sacrifice he paid, which itself is anchored in the sacrificial system of the Old Testament. Death is overturned, which reminds us of the fundamental problem addressed by the Bible's plotline ever since Genesis 3. Water without cost harks back to Isaiah 55; many of the symbolic elements in these chapters are suggestive of Eden before the fall. The constant use of the number twelve picks up twelve Old Testament tribes and twelve New Testament apostles, bringing together all the people of God. No longer will there be any curse here (see Rev. 22:3), which brings to an end the curses imposed in Genesis 3. And I have barely scratched the surface.

Practical Suggestions

First, because apocalyptic literature in general and this passage in particular boast such rich symbolism, it is especially important for leaders to take a little time to peruse a commentary or two. This is not because you will want to dump endless new material on participants in the study but so that you will be prepared to answer questions. Although in this book I have up to now avoided recommending specific commentaries, in this case I shall make an exception. An excellent all-around commentary on Revelation is the one by Robert H. Mounce titled *The Book of Revelation*. If you are an advanced student of the New Testament, you will already be familiar with the authoritative commentary by G. K. Beale (also titled *The Book of Revelation*).

Second, as the section above on theological and pastoral reflections suggests, this is an excellent place to bring many of the strands of the whole Bible together, linking them to Jesus and his gospel, to the culmination of all things in the new heaven and the new earth.

Third, pastorally this material must foster hope and anticipation. They are in short supply when people are going through deep waters. Christian hope is anchored in the past, in what Christ has done, especially in his cross and resurrection, in function of the plan of the Triune God from before the beginning of time, even as it projects into the future, prompting converted men and women in every generation to meld their voices together and cry, "Amen. Come, Lord Jesus" (Rev. 22:20).

Notes

Introduction

1. The article was first published in *The Atlantic* for July/August 2008 and is available at http://www.theatlantic.com/magazine/archive/2008/07/is-google -making-us-stupid/6868/.

2. *Modern Reformation* 17, no. 2 (March/April 2008): 18–23.

3. *Journal of the Evangelical Theological Society* 51 (2008): 813–27.

4. Craig's thirty-page essay is published by Christ on Campus Initiative (2010) and available at http://tgc-documents.s3.amazonaws.com/cci/Craig.pdf.

5. DVD directed by Darren Doane and distributed by LEVEL4, 2009.

6. The comment is cited in many places: e.g., Alister McGrath, *The Unknown God: Searching for Spiritual Fulfilment* (Grand Rapids: Eerdmans, 1999), 23.

7. The April 2, 2009 essay is readily accessible at http://www.newstatesman .com/religion/2009/04/conversion-experience-atheism.

8. One should note that this was not a conversion to *Christian* theism but to a belief in God of a rather deist sort (the distinction is sorted out in chapter 3 of *The God Who Is There*).

Chapter 1 The God Who Made Everything

1. To cite just one view that has appeared since the *Three Views* book, see John H. Walton, *The Lost World of Genesis One: Ancient Cosmology and the Origins Debate* (Downers Grove: InterVarsity, 2009). Walton holds that the opening chapters of Genesis are not concerned with the material origin of the cosmos but with its functions.

2. See also her useful essay on the status of origins-of-life experiments, "Materialism and the Origin of Life," *kategoria* 12 (1999): 41–60 (now also available as a CD-Rom from http://www.matthiasmedia.com.au/kategoria-cd-rom, and shortly to be available online at www.thegospelcoalition.org), and her essay "I Believe in Nature: An Exploration of Naturalism and the Biblical Worldview," published by Christ on Campus Initiative (2008) and available at http://tgc-documents .s3.amazonaws.com/cci/Birkett.pdf.

Chapter 2 The God Who Does Not Wipe Out Rebels

1. The book was published by Eerdmans in 1994. The essay "Sin: Not the Way It's Supposed to Be" is published by Christ on Campus Initiative (2010) and available at http://tgc-documents.s3.amazonaws.com/cci/Pantinga.pdf.

2. *The Briefing* 363 (December 2008): 10–13.

3. *kategoria* 21 (2001): 33–49.

4. *Letter to a Christian Nation* (New York: Knopf, 2006), 26.

Chapter 3 The God Who Writes His Own Agreements

1. The essay was first published in *Themelios* 29, no. 3 (2005): 27–36, but the entire series of *Themelios* publications is available without cost at www.thegospel coalition.org.

Chapter 4 The God Who Legislates

1. See, for instance, Sylvain Romerowski, "Old Testament Sacrifices and Reconciliation," *European Journal of Theology* 16, no. 1 (2006): 13–24.

Chapter 5 The God Who Reigns

1. Andrew Bain, "An Apology for Imperialist Apologetics," *Case* 14 (2008): 24.

Chapter 6 The God Who Is Unfathomably Wise

1. Peter J. Leithart, *Solomon among the Postmoderns* (Grand Rapids: Brazos, 2008), 69.

Chapter 7 The God Who Becomes a Human Being

1. Both essays are published by Christ on Campus Initiative: Craig L. Blomberg, "Jesus of Nazareth: How Historians Can Know Him and Why It Matters" (2008), is available at http://tgc-documents.s3.amazonaws.com/cci/Blomberg.pdf; and Harold A. Netland, "One Lord and Savior for All? Jesus Christ and Religious

Diversity" (2008) is available at http://tgc-documents.s3.amazonaws.com/cci/ Netland.pdf.

2. The book has been published in many editions. This quotation is taken from *The Works of Thomas Hardy in Prose and Verse*, vol. 2, pt. 3 (London: Macmillan, 1918), 254.

Chapter 8 The God Who Grants New Birth

1. Charlotte Brontë, under the pseudonym Currer Bell, in the second edition (1848) of *Jane Eyre*. The preface is most readily read online: http://www.literature .org/authors/bronte-charlotte/jane-eyre/preface.html.

Chapter 9 The God Who Loves

1. See, for example, Michael P. V. Barrett, *Love Divine and Unfailing: The Gospel According to Hosea*, The Gospel According to the Old Testament (Phillipsburg, NJ: Presbyterian & Reformed, 2008).

D. A. Carson teaches New Testament at Trinity Evangelical Divinity School and serves as president of the Gospel Coalition. He is the author of numerous books.

COMPANION
BOOK

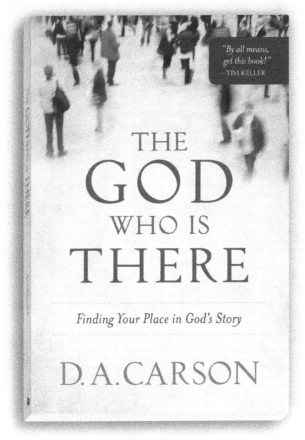

9780801013720 • 240 pp.

"Don Carson's *The God Who Is There* is a unique and important volume in many ways. It is neither a traditional systematic theology nor a Bible survey. It unpacks the whole biblical storyline through the lens of God's character and actions. As a ministry tool, it can be used for evangelism, since it so thoroughly lays out the doctrine of God, as Paul does on Mars Hill in Acts 17. And yet it also does what the catechisms of the Reformation churches did: give Christians a grounding in basic biblical beliefs and behavior. By all means, get this book!"—**Tim Keller**, pastor, Redeemer Presbyterian Church, New York City

BakerBooks
a division of Baker Publishing Group
www.BakerBooks.com

CPSIA information can be obtained
at www.ICGtesting.com
Printed in the USA
FSHW010610140721
83223FS